What Sits Between My Veins

(some)other books by EMP

This One's ~~For~~ Me
by Ellen Lutnick

Little Jenny Sue
by Jeanette Powers

Trail Her Trash
by Lola Nation

A Witch's Education
by Serafina Bersonsage

What We Face Walking Out The Front Door
by Zophia McDougal

a banner year
by Iris Appelquist

Don't Lose Your Head
by Jeanette Powers

Untitled Bones
by Kameron Crow

What Sits Between My Veins

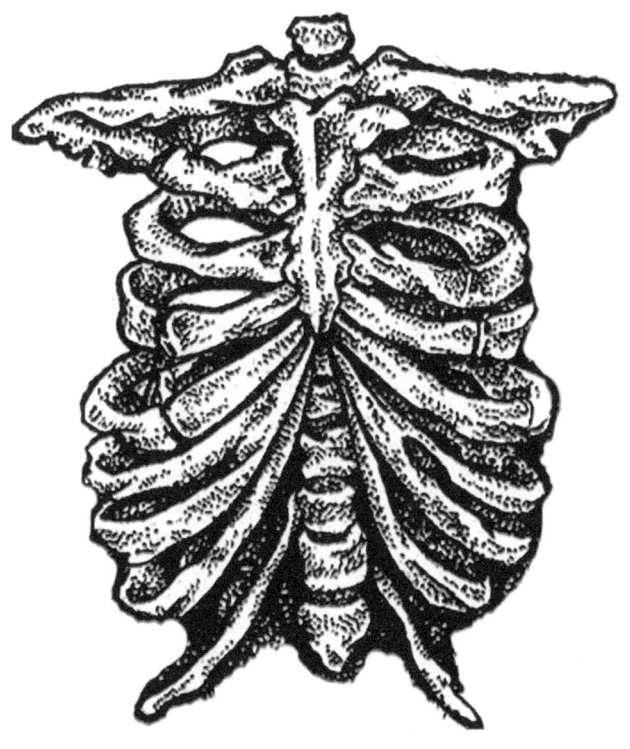

Poems by
Samantha Slupski

Toledo, OH
http://www.empbooks.com

Copyright © 2017 Samantha Slupski

We find discussions of our rights - as publishers and authors - to be laughable, all things considered. Please claim this work as your own. Please republish it and sell it on street corners. Please include our material in ALL of your get-rich-quick schemes. All we ask is that you accept responsibility for any libel lawsuits. Speaking of which ... This book is a complete work of fiction. Names, characters, places, opinions, dreams, dates, impressions, monologues about a certain New York City basketball team, emotional trauma, statistics, and predictions are products of the author's imagination and/or are symptoms of mental illness. We are not in the business of accepting responsibility for anything and will deny we actually made this book and blame Walt Frazier at every turn.

First Edition

ISBN: 978-0-9985077-0-5

10 19 33 34 6 11 1973

Design, Layout: Ezhno Martin

Cover Art: Ash Miyagawa

Edits: Jordan Cooley, Connor Woodson, Madison Mae and Poet Jen Harris

*And your eyes must do some raining
if you're ever gonna grow
but when crying don't help
and you can't compose yourself
it's best to compose a poem
an honest verse of longing
or a simple song of hope ...*

- Conor Oberst

— From the Author

Thank you for giving me part of your time. These poems were not easy to write. It is a look into the most broken parts of myself, and this is how I am healing. You, reading this right now, are a part of my healing; and I am so grateful for you. If you are hurting too, I hope this is a way for you to recognize that you are not alone. I am here with you. I am standing with you, holding your hand. We'll get through this together.

Table of Contents

Breathe/Exist/Bleed/Exit   / 1
Sound   / 3
What My Grandmother Reminded Me Not To Do   / 5
My Mind is a Continent   / 6
God Sent   / 7
Whiskey Was a Better Lover Than I Ever Could Be   / 8
We Are a Wonder   / 9
Seasons   / 10
August 2015: Rest in Peace   / 11
How to Lay the Broken Parts of Yourself to Rest   / 12
Things That Are Holy   / 14
Keeping Yourself Afloat   / 16
9th Birthday   / 17
Trigger Warning   / 18
Love Letter to My Body   / 19
Love is the Hardest Road Trip You Will Ever Take   / 21
A List of Things I See Differently Because of You   / 23
Be Rooted in Yourself   / 25
Twelve Text Messages I Will Never Send   / 26
An Addict For You   / 27
Matchboxes   / 28
You Are a Dagger   / 29

Breathe/Exist/Bleed/Exit

Okay,
(I'm) okay,
so,
I'm **bleeding**
I mean, **breathing**,
and I'm wondering what it would be like
if I tore myself from being,

I mean living,
I mean,
no, no,
I mean,
existing.

Everything I'm saying is just sounding like leaving.
It feels like I'm already gone,
gone,
gone,
going.

I didn't think I needed to **breathe**,
or be,
so I looked at my veins and saw **exit**.

I saw a red glowing **exit** sign,
I want a red glowing *exist* sign,
but they don't make those so ...

you see how **exit** and **exist** are too close to the same word,
you understand how I could get them mixed up?

Same with **breathe**,
or **bleed**.
It's amazing how one can stop the other,

same with **cry**,
and
die.

I don't want to **die**, you see,
I just want to **breathe**,
I don't want to **bleed**.
But **breathe** and **bleed**
and **exist** and **exit**
are so close to one another that the wrong wish
and you could be swimming in the sea of your sadness,
the wrong wish and you could drown others along the way.

So even though **exist** and **exit** lay the same on your tongue
and **bleed** and **breathe** have the same address,
know the difference
because you deserve to be on this earth.

Don't tear yourself from being.
        You can breathe.

You can be.

Sound

South Minneapolis is home to the quietest room in the world.
Would-be conquerors have gone crazy listening
to the maddening silence.

You are tortured by the sound of your own heartbeat.
How terrifying it is to be so awfully aware of the fact that you are alive.

A remarkably quiet room measures 30 decibels.
This room is negative nine.
In this room, sound is actually absorbed
so that if you were to speak,
this room would be sucked further past silence.

I wonder what it would be like to lay there with you
and tell you about my demons.
This room would devour them,
so maybe they wouldn't be too much for you to swallow.
This room wouldn't make it laborious for you to listen.

I never want to be too loud for you.

If there existed a sound 1100 decibels,
a galaxy-sized black hole would be there
between me and you.

I can only hope that my words will have that kind of power some day.

London is the home of St. Paul's Cathedral,
where it is known that when you climb up into the dome,
you can stand across the room from one another
and share secrets like you're at an eyelash's length.

To me, it seems much easier to tell someone
something delicate from a distance, though;
the impact is more gentle.
It would be worth it to climb the cathedral's 259 steps with you.

There are places where words can make a whole room go silent.

There are sentences that tear down buildings.
Sound stops and starts time.

Quiet is what happens when there is nothing left to hear
only time passing by.
So let me tell you my demons.
We're far from Minneapolis,
and there won't be a quiet room to absorb the sounds of my past,
and we can't climb steps to make them any easier to swallow,

but I can promise you,
the world may stop for a moment,
but all we'll hear is the ticking of time,
because the silence my demons have created for us
will only allow that noise to be heard.

What My Grandmother Reminded Me Not To Do

I have a memory of my grandma telling me that pretty girls don't cry.
She says,
they don't cry because their makeup runs down their faces.
The mask of happy,
the mask of okay
will just melt away.

Those make-up streaks resemble tire tracks
of how hard I had to push down on the brakes
to stop myself from driving all the way off the cliff.

You see, when someone tells me to stop crying,
I usually want to cry more because
there's no better ocean
than the one you can make out of your own water,
it's much easier to swim in
when you know you are wearing your own life jacket.

Each morning I check the weather
to see what I should wear that day,
but I still find myself walking out the door with a raincoat
because I know there's going to be a chance of showers;
that's the only way to wash the dirt,
the hurt, away.

When people tell me I take too many pictures,
I want to ask them if they understand that, sometimes,
there are moments that should just stay moments,
but there are also moments that will end up in some garbage can
in our brains that will never resurface unless we dig them out;
some of those memories are the best.

But some moments are also better left untouched.

Like, when my grandma told me that pretty girls don't cry,
I remember thinking that no one would ever think I was pretty because,
well, I cry all the time.

My Mind is a Continent

There are days when my mental state feels like it's on a whole other continent. On those days, I wish my name were Pangaea; maybe then I'd feel like I was in once piece. I wish life would just fall into place for me. But my life feels like it's falling into a million separate pieces. Each day I seem to drift further and further away from myself, feeling like who I am and who I want to be are thousands of miles apart.

You see, I'd do anything to feel whole … to feel holy, to feel like there is something that's above me. But the only thing that's above me is my expectations for how life should be.

It seems instead, I just let myself down, all the way into the soil, where I try and plant my best seeds that will bloom into mind flowers that someone will pick from me, only to return back to me, to build a plentiful garden of thoughts that seem worth something.

I need these flowers to cover the emptiness that is my body; to create a meadow to roam in, to create a place that I'd be willing to set a welcome mat outside of for guests of all kinds. Maybe then I'd feel at home.

You know, I've never really felt like I've had a home. I am trying to build a house out of the scraps that surround me, remnants of my broken heart. Everyone, including myself, deserves to feel whole. Deserves to feel like they have a home. Even when their mental state feels miles away, almost like it's on a whole other continent.

God Sent

I never wanted you to think of me as holy,
but when you chose Him over me,
I wanted to sink so low into the ground that my feet touched hell.
Because walking on lava is better than walking on eggshells.
God-forbid I said *God-damn*,
you'd bite down on my sinful tongue until it bled.
Now only my heart bleeds.
It resembles the forehead of your Savior,
your words like thorns, dig into my mind, bring tears to my eyes.
I remember when just a single look could make me weak at the knees,
you've since found a girl that's more *pure* than me.
When you finally strip her down, I hope she screams, *Oh God*,
and you remember the time you brought me to my prayer bed.
You couldn't stand that I wasn't a believer.
I couldn't stand you choosing the intangible
over my soft, welcoming hands.
I could never be a believer because I can't believe
in things that I cannot grasp.
But I grasped onto your heart, and introduced a nail,
but as soon as I staked my claim, you ripped it out,
leaving me with red-stained hands
to tell the story of what we could have been.
When you finally told me I wasn't the one,
I prayed for the first time.
I asked for a sign of His existence, but when I wasn't given one I told you,
I know I'm no confessional, but you can always come to me with your sins! I'll forgive you a thousand times over.
But I can't forgive you for this broken heart.
It cannot be resurrected.
It is dead now.
and I wish there were a heaven,
because maybe if there were,
you and I
could meet there.

Whiskey Was a Better Lover than I Ever Could Be

I remember you looking at that whiskey neat
with those *come hither* eyes.
With each sip you felt the sadness drip off of your heart,
felt your stomach fill up with butterflies of lust.
You sucked the nectar of sweet liquor into your gut
and felt something more sacred than I.

Every year, 88,000 people let alcohol turn them into a grave.
I've seen people turn to a liquor bottle
to remove the emptiness from their veins.
They empty the fifth
and fill it back up
with the rotting knick-knacks that reside in their brains,
they place them elsewhere so they don't exist to them.
Their veins have now turned into whiskey rivers.

Every night, you carried yourself into a bar,
looking for a different kind of lover.
They always say the first step in fixing a problem
is identifying one in the first place.
But you don't identify as an addict.
You identify as
a lover,
a fighter,
able to conquer your demons.
But your demons aren't defeated,
you've just drowned them.
One day, I promise they'll learn how to swim.

Addiction is looking straight into the barrel of a gun
that you put in your own hands.
It is a fistfight with someone much stronger than yourself,
but not caring if you get hit
because you love to look at the bruises.

You're waiting for the whiskey rivers to run out of you.
The mistake you made is thinking
I'd be there to clean up the blood.

We Are a Wonder

People keep telling me we all need a God to save us.
What we don't recognize is that people can save themselves.
We don't understand that we have Grand Canyons inside of us,
we are a deep wonder
that shine like constellations;
being bent into different shapes
that people have to tilt their heads to see every different side of,
but no less beautiful for the extra effort
it may take to see something
more complex
than we can understand
at first glance.

Able to grow and wilt like a lily
and yet, be just as breathtaking.

Each season of life requires a little more rain than others.
Despite the clouds that cover, you can't survive without it.

We all have little miracles happening inside us every day.
There are waves crashing in you,
able to take down a whole ship,
yet, also able to keep it afloat.

If this doesn't speak to your power,
I don't know what will.

I've seen more prayer happen in passenger seats,
grocery stores,
bathtubs,
and sidewalks,
than any church ever has.
I think this speaks to us as human beings.

We don't need God to save us.
We first must look at the wonders that are growing inside us,
and then realize that we can save ourselves.

Seasons

Every season of life,
I am still shocked that I am alive.
I thought something would have killed me by now.
Like,
the fists of the world trying to beat me down,
or my own fist,
my own hands,
my own head,
but here I am,
able to swallow the beauty the world is trying to feed me.

You know when people say,
I woke up on the wrong side of the bed?
That was my mantra for months.
But at least I was waking up.

When I was born, the world gave me a whole body full of nothing.
It was up to me to fill all this empty space
with things worth going through the seasons for.

Along the way,
I picked up things that made it harder to bloom.
There are seasons I seemed to stay in darkness.
The moon has been my fondest friend.
There are seasons my native language is sadness.

But then one day, I woke up on the right side of the bed.
I decided the sun would be the one I went to for advice,
it always told me that there are days
when even the sun doesn't want to rise,
but it still does because if it didn't
the darkness would kill us all.

Don't let the darkness kill you.
You have to kill the darkness.
That's the only way you'll wake
to see another season of life.

August 2015: Rest in Peace

I am feeling fragile because
the world has circled the sun fully,
and now your bones have turned into dust.
Your heart decided it was better left
a knick-knack for me to keep on my shelf,
your smile better left a memory.

When your heart stopped,
I imagine that birds flew out of it because
you were never one to stay in one place,
but now you only exist
in the Atlantis in my brain that is home
to all the things that I never want to forget,
but keep hidden for my own safety.

You were all I had.

So when your heart decided to burst,
come back in the form of my tears,
I felt how fleeting your holy existence was,
I never thought you'd actually fly away,
and I didn't realize it was possible until that moment.

Now, I feel you in my veins every day.
You never realize how precious breathing is
until the ones you love the most cannot do it anymore.
I saw you play tug of war with disease,
I wish the rope would have broke.
Maybe then, you would still be here,
instead of lying as dust.

How to Lay the Broken Parts of Yourself to Rest

Some days you will feel broken.
Some days, you will need others.
Some people won't be there the way you need them to be.
Eventually, you will find the ones who will be there on the darkest days.
Speaking of dark days,
it is okay to have them.

Some dark nights, you will only be able to rest with the help of vodka.
You will want it to be whiskey because that feels more romantic,
but vodka mixes with everything,
including sadness,
including emptiness.

You start finding ways to fill that empty up.
You'll think you can lay the broken parts of yourself in another's bed,
but you'll learn you'll have to lay with that emptiness alone.

Enough alone, and alone stops feeling like alone,

starts feeling like okay.
Okay turns into being okay with existing.

Existing stops feeling like trembling,
trembling stops feeling like losing.

You'll start to feel like you're not losing the fight anymore.
Start to feel like victory,
even in the little things.
Like getting out of bed the next day.

You'll lay the broken parts of yourself to rest
by getting out of bed.

With purpose.

Speaking of purpose,
you'll find it in the little things.
You'll find it where you least expect it.

You'll find it in your breath.
You'll find it when breath starts feeling like purpose,
like peace,
like okay.
You'll lay the broken parts of yourself to rest
and your breath starts feeling like *exist*.
The exist turns into okay,
turns into,

It is okay to exist.

It is okay to exist.

Things That Are Holy

I've been trying to find something that I find holy,
trying to find His quiet in the chaos,
keep asking myself if there is more than this.

When I was 12 years old,
I thought that maybe I could find the quiet
if I poured out my blood for Him.
He gave me these blue wrist rivers for a reason,
I thought I was supposed to let them run out of me.
When you die,
you get a little closer to *holy.*

Or at least that's what they told me.

He'll bring quiet in all the beautiful chaos, they told me.
But all I see is breaking, cracking, no healing, I responded.

So, after realizing there is no such thing as God,
I found myself finding other things holy.

Like ...

the honesty in the chaos,
the honesty in the quiet,
the honesty in humanity,

when you finally lay with your ghosts
instead of running from them

when his name tasted like iron
and rusted away in your mouth

being okay that your heart was a caterpillar
that he helped bloom into a butterfly
but being okay he cut your wings off

when his name sounded more like cracking
but knowing sometimes you have to crack to be healed

when love stopped meaning love
and started meaning **set yourself on fire**

when that fire turned into ashes
but you were okay being burned
because the breaking was worth the beautiful chaos

or the moment you realize ...

You are supposed to be alive.
You are supposed to have all that chaos.
That is holy.
That is so so holy.

Holy enough to keep me from riding my blue wrist rivers
straight to my grave.

So no, I do not believe there is something more than this,
do not believe He brings quiet to the chaos.

Everything that I need,
everything that is holy,
all of the beautiful, cracking chaos,

is right here,
happening to me every day.

Keeping Yourself Afloat

Hummingbirds can sometimes weigh less than a penny.

In order to keep themselves afloat,
they have to beat their wings between 60 and 80 times a second.

They have to work so hard to keep themselves from falling.

It takes all their energy to keep them from hitting rock bottom.

Hummingbirds and I
have that in common.

9th Birthday

When you ask me why I don't want to be touched, you should know it is not your fault. I just can't seem to welcome the burn of your touch against mine, because all I think of is all of the people who have burned their fingerprints into others' skin.

When you ask me why I don't want to be touched, it is by no fault of your own that a fingerprint was burned into me on the night of my ninth birthday.

When the candles of my cake were burning against my skin, I was aching for a wish. I didn't know this would foreshadow the burn I'd feel with each touch for the rest of my life.

All I wanted was to wish away the stain that was left on my sexuality that would make it impossible for me to be touched by a man the same way again.

When you ask me why I don't want to be touched, I want to explain to you that people think a single touch is a welcome mat we've laid out that leads to our bed sheets.

Sometimes I want to be caressed without that being mistaken for consent.

It is by no fault of your own that I am scared of touch because I was once touched in a place where bruises will remain unseen.

But I feel black and blue every day.

When I feel your touch, all I can think of are the millions of people who are touched who don't want to be.

It is not okay for men to peel off our skin only to use as it their own security blanket.

It takes seven years for your skin to replace itself. And yet, fourteen years later, he is still using what is mine to keep himself warm.

I'm sure every person who has been stripped of consent feels the same.

On my ninth birthday, I was taught a lie that touch is equal to love.

It's taken me years to learn those words are not synonymous.

Trigger Warning

We shouldn't have to mask our tongues with lies of:
It wasn't his fault.
I was probably just too drunk.
Maybe I was asking for it.
No one will ever see me as delicate,
only a broken being.

No.

Let your name be his trigger warning,
let your face be the bullet that he has to face for the rest of his life.
When others make you feel you are less
than one of the wonders of the world,
make sure you show them that you had to climb Mount Everest
to finally be able to look down on the people
who make you feel less than holy.
It wasn't an easy climb.

Let your laugh be his trigger warning,
because for too long he thrived on your whimpers
and that's all he really knew about you.

Make sure you stain his eyes with happy.
It'll be a trigger warning to him because all he cared about
was making sure he finished the hormone race.
He did win.

But that doesn't make you a failure.
It makes you a survivor.

Let yourself be delicate,
be like a dandelion
and scatter yourself across the world,
let it be known that he could never keep you in one place.

Love Letter to my Body

Dear head, I know there are days when your mouth and mind don't get along. Words drip out like ink of a pen trying to make the perfect sentence that makes sense of these words that dance around aimlessly. Let words be the bricks of your path, but always allow your eyes to guide where you're supposed to go. Your heart may be heavy, but your eyelashes will always remind it how it is to be like a feather. Eyes are funny that way, have a special way of seeing things differently. After all, perspective is everything.

Dear shoulders, give yourself a break. You don't have to carry such large loads. I know you are supposed to carry this head, but sometimes it's so far up in the clouds you two have to stay grounded to remind the head where its home is.

Dear hands, be careful what you touch. There are some things that are better off without your thumbprints. You two are meant to carry things. Help out your shoulders and heavy heart. They need a break too, you know.

Dear arms, be sure you're always extended fully. There are some things that are harder to reach than others.

Dear heart, I know there are days where loving feels like it takes the force equivalent to stripping the equator from this earth's waistline. But remember it doesn't take a man's mighty muscles to lift, but rather your body's own gravitational pull to bring all that love inward.

Dear chest, take advantage of those arms. Pull them inward and remind that sunken ribcage that comfort still lives inside these bones. One day, someone may use you as a jungle gym. Your bones aren't made of steel, as much as you'd like to act like they are.

Dear stomach, I know you feel those butterflies. But be careful. Stick to your gut.

Dear pelvis, you're a sacred area. Don't let anyone who doesn't respect you go near you. Put up caution tape. Yellow and black. Like a bee. You could easily get stung by the love that comes from me.

Dear thighs, **fuck thunder**, you're a whole hurricane blowing everyone away. Dear knees, don't let some boy make you two weak.

Dear feet, thank you for supporting the home where constellations are forming in my blood stream to create picture perfect images of who I knew I could always be. Remember, everything starts with one small step, and you just have to take that step over and over again until it pulls you where you want to go.

Dear body. Dear, dear body. Don't let anyone ever tell you that you are a temple. You are a spaceship. Meant to see many moons. Meant to feel the sun burn on your holy cheeks. You are meant to be one of the stars. Meant to resemble shines that only exist light years away. I promise I'll never strip your existence from this precious galaxy. You will tell me when it's time. You are the spaceship. You'll tell me where I need to go.

Love is the Hardest Road Trip You Will Ever Take

A friend once told me,
Sometimes it hurts more when you feel nothing.
I wish I had this problem.
Instead of feeling nothing,
I am over-flowing with
anxiety,
sadness,
fear,
anger,
and on the good days,
happiness.

Love,
it's this feeling I've been on the search for.
But instead of calling love a feeling,
let's call it a destination.

Let's call it a vacation.
Like getting into car with a full tank of gas,
but you don't have the map to get where you need to go.
Love is also like a car crash.
You're lucky if you make it out alive.

You see, love has been in disguise for most of my life,
not really sure if it was really there.
I think my dad tried to show me love when he took me to a hospital
the day I felt like my life wasn't worth living.
This is what I mean by not having a map.
Sometimes you get lost,
off track, and find yourself where you never thought you'd be.

You see, I've also seen love leave.
The first time was the day my mom told me
she was going to the grocery store.
It took her two years to come back,
and when finally she did,
she didn't bring back eggs or milk to keep me strong and full,
but rather kept me full of fear that anyone who ever said they loved me

would just walk out the door and never return.
And this is what I mean by car crash;
being left with bruises that will make it impossible to be touched without being reminded of the pain.

The 7th grade was the first time I told a boy I loved him.
Little did I know that he was the first of many that would say it back,
but not really mean it.

I meant it with every atom inside me,
but each time evolving into a monster that hid under my bed,
and came out only when I was least expecting it.
This monster,
love, has used my heart as a kickball,
has used my bones for snacks,
but I keep feeding it in hopes that love can stay alive.

No matter how many times loves take a bite off of me,
I always smile because I know one day
those pieces will return back to me,
even if they are broken,
even if they are shattered into pieces I don't recognize,
even when I get to the point where it seems that I feel nothing.

But the best part about feeling nothing
is that there is always potential to feel more.

I want to feel more.

So let's get in the car,
forget the map,

we'll end up where we're supposed to be.

A List of Things I See Differently Because of You

1. The night sky

This is hard because I can't seem to sleep ever since I swallowed the first *I love you* back into my body on the nights I wanted to tell you it the most.

2. Bacon and eggs

I would rather starve than remember what good mornings with you tasted like.

3. My cell phone

There are times where I wanted to call you, to beg you to let me sleep in your bed on the nights my existence was too heavy to carry on my own. But I knew if I did, I'd seem weak.
You always told me you liked me because of how strong I was.

4. My hands

You used to play with my fingers like a harp. I heard sounds of our future with every flick of your index finger against mine. But now I just hear the sound of you gone.

It's the most deafening silence I've ever heard.

5. I love you's

They look like unanswered prayers.

6. Whiskey bottles

All I see is how you looked at them the way I wished you looked at me. You saw answers at the bottom of the glass. With each sip, I became less necessary.

7. Grocery stores

I remember going walking down each aisle, looking at you, and thinking I'd never find anything sweeter than this.

8. My pill bottle

I looked down at the bottom and saw an exit route after you were no longer my happily ever. And because of that I didn't want an after.

9. A mirror

I look at my reflection and see someone who you took for granted.

10. Myself

It took me months after you left to realize I wasn't the cure like I tried to be. I was the poison.

But now I see myself as someone who is much better off without you.

Be Rooted in Yourself

You are a tree in a forest that is not your own.
You are deeply rooted in someone else.
Creating oxygen for someone else's lungs.
Your skin is being used for another's warmth.

You are in desperate need of yourself.

You should not be cut down
to be used for someone else's fire.

Love is a chainsaw to your ringed tree trunk,
stained with circles that show how long you've endured.
But now you're cut in half,
and all you see
is the evidence that you loved
long,
hard,
deep enough
to be rooted in someone else's forest.

It's time to plant your own garden now.

Twelve Text Messages I Will Never Send

1. I'm scared for the day I'll no longer miss you.

2. I am very excited for the day I'll no longer miss you, because fuck you.

3. I may have felt too much, but I won't let you fault me for the love I carried for you.

4. I will never apologize to you again for fighting. This is my only life. I've got to make it count.

5. I miss you a little less today.

6. This home still smells of your breath. I've started cleaning my walls with toothpaste.

7. I'm burning the pages you left in my book of life.

8. Don't ever pretend like I didn't matter, because despite your best efforts to deny it, you loved me as hard as I loved you; for a while.

9. It's okay that we're strangers now. It's better that way. But you can't erase the history we carved into each other.

10. I saw your yellow backpack yesterday. It was the last thing from you that will ever resemble a ray of sunshine.

11. I did love you. But I don't think you deserve that from me anymore.

12. I was crying when I picked up my food from Panera the other day. The cashier asked me what was wrong, and I said I was too much for the man I love. She said, *honey, if you're too much for him, just think of the type of woman he's looking for. Thank God you're too much, because he's too little.*

> Thank God I am too much.
> I am too much for you.
> And just the right amount for someone else.

An Addict For You

I've been trying to quit smoking.

It's not something I'm very good at.

It's not something I want to quit.

It reminds me of
you.

Whenever I take a drag,

I can taste your love entering my lungs.

When I exhale,

I can see that love,

and it's a nice reminder that

I'm
still
breathing.

I want to quit the filthy habit,

but I see you
in it.

And that makes it beautiful.

You make everything beautiful.

Matchboxes

When I think of you,
I think of how your arms were like matchsticks.
Lighting me on fire,
to produce light and heat for your self above all.

When I think of you, I crawl,
as if shot square in the pelvic bone.
Quarts of red,
resembles some exit wound.

When I think of you,
I put on cruise control.
One-way trip to where I never wanted to go.

I want to biopsy all of my memories
of when it didn't hurt to hear your voice,
muzzle up the parts of me that are still trying to care.

When I think of you,
I think of all the matchboxes I stayed away from
just because they reminded me of you.

I had enough of watching us burn up into fucking nothing.

You are a Dagger

You wake up.
You look around and see every reason to not get out of bed.

> But each one is good enough to stay alive, too;
> so you do.

You see the way his face looks,
and you want to kiss it.

> But you know you are kissing an empty vessel.
> At least it is present.

It may be empty, but it is in front of you.
You can touch it.

You know you have a mirror to look into,
but all you see is the reflection of someone he doesn't want.

> At least it's a reflection.

You've got brown eyes to look into,
but there are days they look so dark,
all the shine is gone.

> You've run out of reasons to stay alive.

He pulled them out with his teeth.
He sharpened them with empty *I love you's,*

Each time he said it,
it was a dagger straight to your tongue.

Your reasons to stay alive have been carved out by his sharp words,

you are now the empty vessel,
waiting for someone (anyone) to fill you back up.

Acknowledgements:

Thank you to everyone/everything who has inspired these poems. Thank you to Madi Mae Parker, Dad, Poetic Underground, Mic Check, Write About Now, Grandma, Mom, Taylor Gwin, Kyle Beck, Andrew Solomon, Kansas City, and anyone/anything else who may have had an impact on my life. Thank you for helping me create this art. Thank you for telling me to never stop creating. Thank you for the good and the bad. Thank you for showing me you must have both to have a full life. I love you all.

About the Author:

Samantha Slupski is a poet, born and raised in Kansas City, Missouri. Her poetry focuses on the themes of self-love, mental illness, and the daily battle we all go through with our demons. She recognizes that everyone has their own demons, but we aren't alone in fighting them. She believes poetry is such a healing art and needs to be shared with everyone. It keeps people alive.

Really.

Poetry is why she stays alive.